MW00762620

COAST OF MAINE, *

IN AND AROUND

KENNEBUNKPORT.

PRICE, FIFTY CENTS.

CTURESQUE NOOKS

ON THE

COAST OF MAINE, *

IN AND AROUND

KENNEBUNKPORT.

PRICE, FIFTY CENTS.

BY H. W. RANKIN,
CH STREET,
Y. CITY.

 Photographed by A. J. Gavett.

RIVER, LOOKING TOWARD VILLAGE.

SCENERY NEAR OCEAN BLUFF

 Ph[illegible] by C. S. [illegible]

UP THE RIVER.

Copyrighted, 1894, by H. W. Rankin. *Photographed by A. J. Gavett.*

A ROCK-BOUND COAST.

 Photographed by A. B. Houdlette.

ST. ANN'S.

Photographed by A. R. Hoadlette.

BLOWING CAVE.

OLD FALLS.

Copyrighted, 189[illegible], H. W. Eaken. *Photographed by C. A. Gatson.*

KENNEBUNK RIVER.

 Photographed by A. J. Gard.

LOOKING TOWARD CAPE PORPOISE, NEAR BLOWING CAVE.

Copyrighted, 1894, by H. W. Rankin. *Photographed by A. J. Gavitt.*

THE LATEST LAUNCH.

 Photographed by A. J. Gavett.

END OF BREAKWATER.

 Photographed by A. J. Garett.

HECKMAN'S DOCK.

 Ph[illegible]aphed by A. B. H[illegible].

SPOUTING ROCK.

 Photographed by A. J. Garett.

KENNEBUNK RIVER AND BOAT CLUB HOUSE.

Copyrighted, [illegible], by H. V. Rankin. *Photographed by A. R. [illegible].*

VIEW SEAWARD FROM DR. CLARK'S GROUNDS.

Trusting the one great Pilot of the deep

To be for aye my tender, low-voiced guide,

I look aloft to Him and say—

Tho' tossed upon life's ocean wide—

All's well! All's well!

By day or night, all's well!

WILLIAM HALE.

CPSIA information can be obtained
at www.ICGtesting.com
Printed in the USA
LVHW082255300320
651714LV00031B/249

9 780342 506255